Ian Waites

# Middlefield

## A postwar council estate in time

*Uniformbooks* 2017

First published 2017
Copyright © Ian Waites
ISBN 978-1-910010-16-7

*Uniformbooks*
7 Hillhead Terrace, Axminster, Devon EX13 5JL
www.uniformbooks.co.uk

Trade distribution in the UK by Central Books
www.centralbooks.com

Printed and bound by T J International, Padstow, Cornwall

"I would like there to exist places that are stable, unmoving, intangible, untouched and almost untouchable, unchanging, deep-rooted places that might be points of reference, of departure, of origin..."

—Georges Perec, *Species of Spaces and Other Pieces*

"Lying in bed, I abandoned the facts again and was back in Ambrosia"

—*Billy Liar*

# Introduction

For the first three years of my life, between 1961 and 1964, I lived in a house along an early-nineteenth century terrace called 'Popplewell's Row'. These days the name might appeal to some as a picturesque, Pickwick-esque, Dickensian period detail. In the early 1960s however, the thought of anything 'Dickensian' rightly condemned places like Popplewell's Row to destruction, as part of "the drive against the slums, to house people in decent homes". I think back to then and imagine a group of planners and councillors in the offices of the Gainsborough Urban District Council flicking through photostat copies of the 'Revised Plan'. They loom over architects' drawings of a new council estate like demi-gods of Modernity, and say things like "the density can only be increased if building takes place in an upward direction". A finger points at a map and traces the line of the then-isolated country road that will give this estate its name: Middlefield Lane.

Now it is May 1964, and my parents and I are viewing what is to be our new home on the estate. Somewhere in the distance a cement mixer churns, creating a metallic loop of sound. My mother pushes the back door open and an audible release of air reverberates through the empty shell of the house, as if it has been hermetically sealed ready for its new tenants. I smell fresh putty and newly planed wood. I see the red and blue dots on the kitchen taps. We step into the house and straight into a small 'utility room'. Later, we put a table and some matching chairs in there, and called it 'the meal room'. The table had a lemon yellow Formica surface covered with black-lined abstract squiggles that I used to obsessively follow with my fingertip. Because it was a cool room, without heating, we had our tea there on hot summer days. The front façade of the house is plain, asymmetrical, and rectilinear (but with the exception of a parabolic concrete canopy over the front door). In addition to the utility room, the house has two bedrooms, a bathroom, a living room, and a kitchen with a pantry. It is unheated apart from an open fireplace in the living room, but it has a bathroom and inside toilet, kitchen 'tops', hot and cold running water, a TV aerial socket, and a 'picture-window'. These things seem almost rudimentary now, but back then we thought they were extraordinary.

The Middlefield Lane estate is representative of the post-World War Two, 'Welfare State' reconstruction of British society and culture: between 1945 and 1969, local authorities built around four million dwellings—some 59% of all housing built over that period. Gainsborough was a small, provincial Lincolnshire market town at the start of the 1960s, with a population of around 17,000 people, but the council was modern, go-ahead, and it was busy carrying out a programme of modernisation across the town. Everything was 'New'. The town centre's dense medieval street patterns were being opened up to accommodate a new parade of shops and a new Guildhall. At the same time, the *Gainsborough Evening News* celebrated Middlefield with the publication of an aerial photograph of the estate under the headline "Take a Look at New Gainsborough". The 'look' of this 'new' world was defined by the clean architectural lines of postwar modernism, and by experimental ideas in planning which aimed to separate the car from the family. My childhood experiences of Middlefield were conditioned by those ideas: the pedestrianised nature of the estate in particular gave its children an enormous amount of space to play in. Its very newness provided them with a blank canvas where a completely new way of life could be created. "Space", someone once said, "is structured differently in juvenile life… It is intensely concerned with paths and boundaries… and other special places for particular things. This whole home range… is, in effect, imprinted."

*Middlefield: A postwar council estate in time* presents an itinerary of those "special places for particular things". It is a guide to the estate's topology, where the outward appearances give expression to its inner life via short textual bursts of historical reportage, sensory experiences, and memories. When I started researching the history of Middlefield a few years ago, I thought I was carrying out memory work. I went back to the estate time and time again in an attempt to think myself back into my childhood and youth there. To some extent this book perpetuates that process, but as it evolved the photographs here began to set their blank, indifferent twenty-first century faces against those memories. Recently I visited the estate to take some photographs of the signs which were put up more than fifty years ago to help visitors find their way around, but my intentions kept being thwarted: a car was parked directly under one sign, the ground before another had been newly fenced off. I went to the site of the communal aerial, but I was hassled by two dogs in a nearby garden that wouldn't stop barking at my presence. A few years ago, there was a distinct 'target' of grass and soil where the circular base of the mast used to be. Now it has virtually disappeared, leaving a dull area of ground that has become difficult to photograph in any meaningful way. The reality of the estate as it is today begins to assert itself, and on its own terms. New families live there now, while children continue to play in the same special places as I did. In a time of housing scarcity, this book reminds us that Middlefield is still here, is still essential, and still growing into something as we remember it.

# Middlefield

*The distant rim*     12

*The Kennedy Estate*     17

*Greens*     18

*Signs*     23

*Maisonettes*     24

*Trees*     29

*The Phosco P107*     30

*The communal aerial*     33

*Pebbledash*     34

*Kerbs*     37

*Cobbles*     38

*Privet*     41

*Cut-throughs*     42

*Friends*     48

*Open Doors*     64

*Peace*     67

*Parks*     68

*Dens*     81

*Bus Stop*     82

*Garages*     85

*The shops*     86

*Field*     91

## The distant rim

The new estate pushed the town further into the countryside. The homes lined up against open fields, and the residents found themselves both at a new end, and a new beginning. Critics of the time looked down upon this type of open development. They imagined unhappy housewives being socially and psychologically marooned on the "distant rim of their sentimental green landscapes... cut off from the neighbourliness of closely built-up streets". This was "Prairie Planning", which could only result in boredom, restlessness, and the rise of some very suburban neuroses.

## The Kennedy Estate

The minutes of a Gainsborough Urban District Council housing committee meeting held in December 1963 show that the committee considered calling the estate "The Kennedy Estate" as a tribute to John F. Kennedy after his assassination. The committee decided however that "no action be taken on this suggestion but that the use of the late president's name be borne in mind when the naming of future recreation grounds or housing estates is under consideration". His name was never used.

## Greens

As he was beginning to think about how Middlefield should look, the estate's architect took his wife out for a Sunday drive to a council housing development in Coventry, so he could experience a Radburn layout at first hand. Back then, planners wrote breezily and proactively about estates like Middlefield: "What we can do in housing schemes is minimise the car's visual intrusion; and, by separating it as completely as possible from pedestrians, keep it from making life dangerous and unpleasant". At Middlefield, cars were kept 'round the back', along short, cul-de-sac, service lanes. On the other side—'the front'—short rows of houses were grouped around open green spaces that were either given modern, functional names (The Green) or which were named after nearby deserted medieval villages (Dunstall Walk). All was for the communal good: "Only then can motorists and pedestrians, who are also sometimes the same people, enjoy the best of both worlds".

TO
PRIORY CLOSE
ODD NUMBERS
THE GREEN
EVEN NUMBERS
SOUTH PARADE
ODD NUMBERS
DUNSTALL WALK

## Signs

Some people fretted about the open plan, pedestrianised nature of Middlefield. As the estate neared completion, the local head postmaster wrote to the clerk of the council about "the problems arising in connection with the delivery of mail on an estate designed on Radburn principles". There were no streets as such, and apparently no one could tell the backs from the fronts of houses, or the odds from the evens. So signs indicating the ways across the estate were provided, even though the arrangement of the blocks of houses still essentially conformed to tradition: odds on one side and evens on the other, but with open green spaces separating the two sides rather than a through road. The residents got it though. They were taking new decisions; they moved to the front. In the old slum terraces, the front door was never used. Everyone used the back door. Now it was different. The residents began to live in the living room, rather than existing in the kitchen.

## Maisonettes

The overall construction of Middlefield was contracted to George Wimpey and Co. Ltd, and the majority of the housing on the estate ended up being designed and built in what was then a typical, often repeated and fairly traditional Wimpey-style. Middlefield's architect, however, had a different vision for the overall look of the estate; he was "keen to keep Wimpey at bay", and wanted "to produce a modern estate". He designed these maisonettes. The children used to think that they were living in Marineville.

## Trees

In the first year of the estate's completion, new concerns were raised, this time about new trees being planted too close to the houses. The architect of the estate was consulted and he responded with his usual single-minded determination to maintain the aesthetic purity of the environment he'd designed, stating that any removal of trees would "upset the balance and layout of the estate". As a consequence, "no action was taken", and the trees still grow there today.

## The Phosco P107

The Phosco P107 lit up the network of footpaths that characterised the estate, and the visual and physical impact of their 'space age' design was never lost on the children as they played. They were a good 'home' for a game of Blocko. The P107 was the local authority lamppost of choice during the 1960s, and they are still being made today in Hertfordshire, that postwar county stronghold of the council estate and new town.

## The communal aerial

In May 1965, the local newspaper announced "A new amenity for Middlefield Lane": a "communal television aerial, installed to serve the entire estate". The 60 foot-high mast was situated within a small triangle of grass, and it stayed there until the late 1980s when it was swept away by a new and increasingly unregulated world of Squarials and individualism: a rough disc of barren ground marks its position today. In the postwar years of paternalistic modernism however, the aerial did more than merely serve the communal good—it was also intended to have an aesthetic effect on Middlefield's environment: "the new aerial scheme... removes the need for individual aerials" reckoned the county surveyor, "and this will give a tidier look to the estate".

## Pebbledash

When the local newspaper reported on the progress of
Middlefield's construction, it called the estate "mushroom
town" because it seemed to spring up overnight. In its early
days though, the estate was more mineral than vegetable:
bricks, sand, putty, and pebbledash were left everywhere. The
houses were built at speed—the external walls were cast in
concrete poured into reusable wooden or steel shutterings,
which were then removed to create a basic shell. After that,
the walls were pebble dashed with small shards of white,
yellow, burnt orange and grey-blue flint and stone. To the
child's microcosmic eye, the colours and the sharp textures
presented a world that was half interesting, half ignorable.
Bored children would huddle by a friend's wall, and while they
talked about what to do next they would absent-mindedly try
to prise pieces off. The fragments would make a little soft snap
as they came away. House-proud parents however generally
disapproved of these tiny acts of vandalism. No matter where
they were within the house, no matter what they were doing,
they would always know when a piece of pebbledash had been
removed, and they would come out and tell the children to
stop it, and to go away and do something else.

## Kerbs

The attempt to minimise the impact of the car on the community was constantly thwarted by the children, who nevertheless created a limitless micro-network of pretend roads and motorways on the estate's kerbs. Day in, day out, they played 'cars' with whatever Matchbox vehicles they could lay their hands on. These children played at ground level, wearing out knees in trousers as they knelt on the ground, or splitting the soles of their shoes as they squatted on the balls of their feet, pushing die-cast vehicles along strings of elongated concrete blocks. Chalk or crayons were used to draw lane markings, parking bays, 'houses' and 'shops' up and down the estate. On a cornerstone, the rules of the road would be observed by drawing some Give Way dotted lines and triangles. The children of Middlefield manip-ulated the planned fabric of the estate to their own desires and needs.

## Cobbles

"Large cobbles hand-pressed into a concrete surface prevent pedestrians and cars from cutting across corners."

## Privet

All the back gardens on the estate used to be defined by privet hedging. They softened the built environment. This hedge must be at least fifty years old now, and it evokes memories of the early days of the estate: the sweet, heady scent of the small creamy white flower buds that more often than not did not come into bloom at all; the damp remnants of an old British Rail national timetable stuffed under the hedge in a friend's garden.

## Cut-throughs

The cut-throughs threaded the estate together, and joined up
the lives of the children who lived there. As they saw their
children disappear into one of those narrow channels of
privet, wall and fence, parents would wonder where they had
been. Where were they going, what were they doing? But,
if asked, the children would have to admit that they didn't
know: we go down there, down there, along there, to there,
or we go that way. As they crossed the estate, constantly
in motion, strolling, running, cycling, they were free from
time. No burdens of the past pressed upon them; nor did
they wonder what the future might hold. In the cut-throughs
they felt both connected and absent-minded. They were in
reverie. The seer and the seen, the child and the place, were
indistinguishable.

## Friends

Patrick wanted to form a reggae band with me even though neither of us could play an instrument (I had a Bontempi organ though).

## Friends

Stephen's family came from Sheffield. One day I called for
him to ask if he could come out to play. His Mum answered
the door and told me, "No, we're having us teas".

## Friends

Mark and I used to listen to The Faust Tapes and Camembert Electrique on his brother's hi-fi.

## Friends

Heather and her family moved away from the estate very quickly.

## Friends

Neil wanted to beat me up one night but his elder brother
Gary stopped him.

## Friends

Darryl's Dad worked for an airline.

## Friends

I remember Patricia:
"Shake your hair girl with your ponytail
Takes me right back (when we were young)
Threw your precious gifts into the air
Watched them fall down."

## Friends

A friend lived here, but I don't remember their name.

## Open doors

When the sun shone down on Middlefield, the front doors would be thrown open to let some warmth and air into the homes. The sun would stream in through the door so bright it made the carpet patterns quiver under its force. People sat out in the sun on their doorstep while kids bombed up and down the footpaths on their bikes.

## Peace

Clocks ticked slowly, Radio 2 wavered in and out from
a tinny battery transistor radio in the kitchen, sparrows
chirped, and—this being Lincolnshire during the 1960s and
70s—the occasional Vulcan bomber grumbled ominously
overhead.

## Parks

"The old park." Swings, roundabout, see-saw. One study
of British council housing schemes built during 1968–69
showed that out of thirty-nine estates specifically intended
for families, only four had parks with play equipment.
Middlefield was different, progressive: in 1965 it already had
two playparks, one on each side of the shopping precinct.
Despite this, in 2011, both of them were inexplicably stripped
of their equipment, leaving behind a set of new, yet suddenly
ancient, earthworks: concentric circles of grass and concrete,
oblongs of blank, disintegrating synthetic play surfaces.

## Parks

"The baby park." This apparatus helps the teenagers on the estate to behave unconventionally. They hang out here, squeezing themselves unreasonably into the swings. They sit on the tiny roundabout and enjoy going around slowly for a change. They don't know it yet, but they are already nostalgic for their easier childhood.

## Parks

"The big park." For 'big', read intermediate, middle, junior. The ten and eleven year-olds play here: they have named all these parks, labelling them for themselves, creating reference points for their future memories. The teenagers don't frequent this park because it's for children.

## Dens

Time slowed down for the children when they were bored and didn't know what to do, and it went by far too quickly when they were out and about on summer mornings, creating a den within overgrown hawthorn bushes on the undeveloped edges of the estate. They would come back a couple of days later to find that someone had trashed it. They would start again.

## Bus Stop

After they had moved onto the new estate, Middlefield's residents stated that they had "few complaints". Above all, they seemed to like what one woman described as the "fresh-air feeling". The "biggest bone of contention" however was the lack of an adequate bus service into town. Soon after, the local bus company introduced a new route that passed by the estate, and a bus stop was created against the end wall of the North Parade flats. The stop consisted of a flat-roofed shelter that stood on a broad paved area built up to the level of the road where the bus stopped. Excited children would become irritable as they waited impatiently with their mums for the bus to arrive. Bored teenagers pressed themselves against the back wall of the shelter to keep out of the rain, which is probably why the shelter was eventually removed.

## Garages

The council originally built 143 garages at Middlefield to cater for a projected increase in car ownership, but they always struggled to be let. Back in the 1960s and '70s, everything was local. People either walked into town or, if it was raining, they got the bus. The car never really flourished on the estate, even into the twenty-first century. In 2012, a number of garages were removed, leaving clean, white rectangles that somehow brightened up the estate, but which also served as a reminder of a future that, for some, never quite took off.

## The shops

M00/P/0767 Consent to demolish flats, shops and grub up all foundations and seal redundant drains.

21/8/2000 1–16 The Precinct (inclusive), Gainsborough.

The Proposal: This application proposes the demolition of this parade of shops with flats above on The Precinct at North/South Parade. The building contains six shop units, five of which are vacant, with ten three bedroom flats above. Only one of the flats is still occupied.

Comment: This application proposes the demolition of this building at The Precinct... as part of ongoing improvement/regeneration work on the Middlefield Lane estate... indicated in a letter of support that these properties have had a long history of low demand, serious vandalism and unlettability [sic]...

In view of the above... and the wish to carry out a proactive role in regenerating and redeveloping the area, it is considered that this demolition work is appropriate and acceptable and helps to open up the centre of this residential area, creating a more pleasant and less enclosed environment.

Recommendation: Grant consent.

## Field

When the people first moved onto the estate in 1964, this field had wheat growing in it. Then the by-pass came, and with it some industrial units, followed by an out-of-town supermarket. Subsequently, the field seemed to shrink; it became cut off, and gradually it fell out of use. Nature has taken over now, and in the summer it becomes full of cow parsley, the field brimming with dozens of skylarks that spiral up and down on the wing, like little Harrier jump jets. The people who live in the houses opposite the field today keep an eye out on the horse that grazes there, and state that they would never want to live anywhere else. One young man in his early twenties says that he likes the quiet—"It's open, I like the space"—much like anyone would have said fifty years ago when they moved onto the estate, far away from the town's slum housing. Then, as he pauses and looks out over the field, his girlfriend shouts that their neighbour has "gone". "Hmm", he mutters, half to the field, half to himself, "mad bitch. Gotta go".

# Notes

p.7 "the drive against the slums…"
*Gainsborough Evening News*, 9 July 1963.

"the density can only be increased…"
Gainsborough Urban District Council
(GUDC) Minute Books, Vol.LXII (1961–62),
Housing Committee Minute No.1377, p.403.

p.8 "between 1945 and 1969…"
M. Glendinning and S. Muthesius, *Tower Block: Modern Public Housing in England, Scotland, Wales and Northern Ireland*.
London: Yale University Press, 1994, p.1.

"Take a Look at New Gainsborough"
*Gainsborough Evening News*, 25 May 1965.

"Space is structured differently in juvenile
life…" Paul Shepard, 'Place and Human
Development.' *Children, Nature, and
the Urban Environment: Proceedings of a
Symposium-Fair*, Washington, D.C., 19–23
May 1975, p.7.

p.12 "on the distant rim…" J. M. Richards,
'Failure of the New Towns', *Architectural
Review*, July 1953, p.32.

"Prairie planning…" Gordon Cullen, 'Prairie
Planning in the New Towns', *Architectural
Review*, July 1953, pp.33–36.

p.17 "The Kennedy Estate". GUDC Minute
Books, Vol.LXIV (1963–64), Housing
Committee Minute No.1007, p.352.

p.18 "the estate's architect took his wife out
for a Sunday drive…" Neil Taylor, telephone
interview with author, 23 March 2012.

"Radburn layout". A model of estate
planning so called because it was based
on the small, unfinished, settlement of
Radburn in New Jersey (1929), which had
been one of a number of experimental
housing projects promoted by the Regional
Planning Association of America at the
time of the Great Depression. The Radburn
layout has been appropriately described
as "garden city plus motor car", because it
was designed to provide dual but otherwise
quite separate circulation systems for cars
(short cul-de-sac lanes that ran off a limited
number of access roads and which would
lead to parking at the back, or "service",
side of the houses) and for pedestrians
(networks of public footpaths and green
spaces kept away from the roads at the
front of the houses). Radburn planning was
first acknowledged in this country in a
1944 housing manual, but came to be more

widely applied to the design and layout of
many English council estates in the 1960s,
when it was envisaged that personal car
use would rapidly increase over the decade.
Ever aware of new ideas and precedents,
Middlefield's architect, Neil Taylor, was
keen to adopt Radburn principles to the
layout of the estate as he began work there
in 1962.

"What we can do in housing schemes…"
Ministry of Housing and Local Government,
*Cars in Housing 1: Some Medium Density
Layouts*, 1966, p.1.

p.23 "problems arising in connection with
the delivery of mail…" GUDC Minute Books,
Vol.LXIV (1963–64), Housing Committee
Minute No.663, p.222.

p.24 "George Wimpey and Co Ltd".
Construction company. By the end of the
1950s, Wimpeys had come to dominate
the British local authority house building
market, producing up to 18,000 council
houses a year. (taylorwimpey.co.uk/about-
us/who-we-are/our-history)

"keen to keep Wimpey at bay". Neil Taylor,
telephone interview with author, 23 March
2012.

"Marineville". A fictitious city from the year
2065 that is home to the headquarters of
the World Aquanaut Security Patrol (WASP).

p.29 "upset the balance and layout of the
estate". *Gainsborough Evening News*, 7 June
1966.

p.30 "Blocko". A children's game, sometimes
also known as "Forty-forty-in". A player is
chosen to be "in", or as "it", and a landmark
such as a tree or lamppost is chosen as
the base. Players who are not "it" run and
hide, while "it" counts to a certain number,
usually 100. "It" looks for the other players,
while the players try to get to base without
being seen. If a player gets to base without
being seen, they shout "blocko one-two-
three myself" (or, more commonly on the
Middlefield estate, "Denno"). They are then
safe, and will wait at base for the remainder
of the game. In order to catch someone, "it"
must see the person, run back, touch the
base and say "blocko one-two-three [name]".
Players that are caught by "it" return to
base. The last person to be caught by the end
of the game is "it" for the next game.

p.33 "A new amenity for Middlefield Lane" *Gainsborough Evening News*, 26 May 1965.

"Squarials". The Squarial (a combination of the words square and aerial) was a satellite antenna used in the 1980s and 90s for the reception of the now defunct British Satellite Broadcasting television service.

p.34 "mushroom town". *Gainsborough Evening News*, 10 September 1963.

p.37 "Matchbox vehicles". Small, die-cast metal toy vehicles, made by Lesney Products from 1953 until 1982, which were sold in boxes similar in style and size to matchboxes.

p.38 "Large cobbles hand-pressed…" Robert Maguire, 'External Pavings 2', *Architectural Review*, April 1957, p.284.

p.48 "Bontempi organ". A low-priced, plastic-cased, brightly-coloured chord organ popular in the 1970s, manufactured by the Italian musical instrument manufacturer, Bontempi.

p.52 'The Faust Tapes'/'Camembert Electrique'. Albums by the progressive rock bands Faust and Gong, which were issued in the UK in 1974 by Virgin Records for the price of a single (59p), a marketing scheme used in the hope that these greatly discounted albums would give more exposure to the artists and encourage sales of their regularly priced works.

p.60 "Shake your hair girl…" Lyrics from 'If there is something' by Bryan Ferry. Recorded by Roxy Music in 1972.

p.67 "the occasional Vulcan bomber". The Avro (Hawker Siddeley) Vulcan was a jet-powered delta wing high-altitude strategic bomber, which was operated by the Royal Air Force from 1956 until 1984 at RAF Waddington and RAF Scampton in Lincolnshire.

p.68 "One study of British council housing schemes built during 1968–69…" Clare Cooper Marcus and Wendy Sarkissian. *Housing as if people mattered.* Berkeley: California University Press, 1986, p.136.

p.82 'The Likes and Dislikes of a New Estate: Middlefield Lane residents have few complaints', *Gainsborough Evening News*, 29 December 1964.

p.85 "143 garages". GUDC Minute Books, Vol.LXIII (1962–63), Housing Committee Minute No.365. p.118.

p.86 'M00/P/0767 Consent to demolish'. West Lindsey District Council. Planning Services Committee Minutes, 18 October 2000.

p.91 "like little Harrier jump jets". The Hawker Siddeley Harrier was a jet aircraft developed in the 1960s, which was capable of taking off and landing vertically.

"One young man in his early twenties…" Conversation with the resident of 44 Dunstall Walk, 4 June 2015.